LIFE

A CONSTANT MOVEMENT

VAISHNAVI RAMESH

Made with ♥ on the Notion Press Platform
www.notionpress.com

"To all the lovable souls who have graced my life in profound ways, igniting flames of understanding, empathy and growth within my being. With heartfelt gratitude for your constant support, inspiration and companionship, I dedicate these words to you".

Contents

Contents

Contents

Preface

Life with all its intricacies, is a mosaic of emotions that shapes our existence.In this book, we embark on a voyage through the landscape of human experience,exploring the depths of our emotions,enthralling the significance of our moments.Through poetry,we navigate through the ebbs and flows of life.Beyond the surface of mere words, lies a deep truth that is beyond language, resonating silently in spaces between.As you delve into these phrases, may you find clarity in the depths of uncertainity.May you explore the infinite capacity of the heart to endure and to love.Joining hands with me on this invincible voyage of life to wander,wonder and reveal the inner beauty of your "Self".

Prologue

This narration begins with whispers of a newborn soul entering into this old world again.Seeks to know the truth beyond all existence.Pleading the source of existence, as host to reveal the reality hidden beneath the journey of life.Follow the pages closely as you may reveal the echoing beats of universe revealing the resonanace in the dance of life.Amidst the chaos and confusion there is a thread of continuity,the thread that binds all of us.Through the verse you will traverse the landscape of human emotions, guided by the steady rhythm of the eternal source that is binding all our souls.

1. MOTHER'S WOMB

Into the womb, where darkness bounds.
Where am I? After few mystical rounds.
So high are the sounds around.
Am I inside a factory ground?
Yet again, entering into the cycle of birth and death.
Beneath the human body and mind.
Wonder! Onto the mighty path one more time.
After lots of wander on the shallow reigns.
Entering into this world with a key chance, once again.
To merge into the reality, through excavation of the self.

2. BIRTH

After a long wait of patience and growth.

Here I come, with a drastic bounce.

Into the exotic world, already known.

But now, new creatures with different faces roaming around.

Holding me upside down.

To check the viability of my birth.

Survival instincts, to gasp my breath afresh.

Out comes a piercing shrill.

Which confirms my life abode.

Those glazing lights around, blurring my sight.

Out in fear, I cry aloud to grip my life on earth.

After few quick cleanses and routines.

Back into my mother's arms with pure bliss.

3. MOTHER

Neither you chose me, nor I chose you.
But both into, the same old drama anew.
And now, I am from you.
Who nurtured me good with your red hue.
Here I am, as a bundle of joy.
Resting on, the long awaited arms uphold.
Tiny moments created now, to be cherished for decades astound.
Though growing old, shall fade my memories away.
Valuing this moment to embark my new journey with you.
Under your boundless showers of love.
Oh mother! My Eternal angel.
Blessed to be born through you.
Oh my Dear Mother! Finally your wish has come true!

4. HUNGER

Here I cry out, in a severe howl.

The need to fill my inner bowl.

Rushing into the game of life?

With multiple emotions flooding at stretch.

I cry out loud, to calm my hunger bells.

The feel is super intricate, as I miss my old golden place.

After all travel, back into the same emotional pain?

When hunger rings, my memory thins.

Becoming quite hard to withhold the golden glimpse.

I'm getting lost when emotions host.

Back into the drama of life as whole.

5. SLEEP AND WAKE

The more I sleep, delving into the growing phase.
My body and mind calms into a resting phase.
Though it is vital for my physical growth.
I could feel an ever ending glow when my eyes are shut.
The same old place where I rested, before this birth.
But now again into the trap of life.
Losing my state of unity.
Everything that takes a form, enters into the mortal norms.
The state of sleep and the wake of hunger.
Stimulating a weird paradoxical flow.
Against my innate nature of existence.
So close to the golden glimpse, hard I spare.
Making it hard to withhold the balance, I dare.
Sleep and wake building new boundaries.
Creating the separation of duality.
Hiding the everlasting oneness with reality.
Hidden beneath every creature.
While sleep charges the body ,wake drains the energy.
Sleep and wake being the my mere experience into duality.
Losing my inner state of reality.
Subsiding into the gravitational pull of life!

6. EMOTIONS

Steeps of emotions flooding here and there.
As a newborn, I weigh so light.
But back into this mortal body, I weigh so high.
Tantrums emerge disturbing my inner state of calm.
My face frown with pain, of losing my eternal abode again.
Former abode ! With an expansion of boundless love.
Now getting constrained within this physical crowd.
But my smile, may lighten up the people's heart.
Though, holding my tiny fingers , brings solace on their heart.
Who have forgotten their inner weightless state!
Living so long, in this mysterious maze.
As I smile, so shall they shy with enormous flow of energy by.
With showers of innocence, blooming their heart.
Taking them back, to their nostalgic past.
The ones who have forgotten their inner happiness.
Bringing them back into the reality of "NOW".
My purpose of life starts with this little count.

7. MY FIRST CRAWL

Here I move with my arms and legs.
Here and there I sit for rest.
Little crawls propelling a vigorous energy flow.
Draining all the stored up energies, making me snore.
People around me, cherishing,my little moves.
Tiny little things seems too great, in their point of view.
The four leg crawl turning into double leg stand.
Everything happening just as a flow.
Coded and embedded within every soul.
All things happening accordingly in a systematic pattern.
The beauty of every creature, inborn with all its precious
features.

8. NATURE

Nature deals with its own pattern of existence.
Expanding into creation followed by destruction,
balancing its own flow of expansion.
A triangular pattern in all the recurring creatures as code.
But the uniqueness lies in its existing source.
Birth and death being the physical extremes life.
That draws each and every creature into cyclic nature.
In between these lies a signicant feature.
Of identifying one's own self, with the highest form of existence.
To make use of the chance given.
To merge body, mind and soul into one.

9. DREAMY STATE

Entering into the dreamy state inbetween wake and sleep.

Where I can sense the hidden real me.

Beyond the conditioned physical beam.

Unto an unconditional mystic spirit within.

One huge question throbbing my emotional dream.

Why am I back again into this physical stream?

After all those hard striving births and deaths.

Back again into this same old path of quest.

Is there not an end to this game of life.

Where mere transformation occurs.

My purest, lovable, highest source! Can you reveal me as host?

10. AN EXTRA DAY TO LIVE

Death being a delightful wakeup, from a giant dream.
After all those hard striving, behind the scenes.
To comprehend and execute the roles of life.
Knowledge driven beneath each and every experience alive.
After all those struggles and chaos around, the moment arrived.
For the final freedom of the illusive self.
To the ultimate source of eternal reality.
At last! Here I am, out of all the physical realm.
All of a sudden! Came an offer.
With an extra day to live life after.
Alas! The purpose not yet fulfilled.
Accepting the offer and returning with will.
Once again plunging into the dark universe abound.
An extra day granted, lengthening into yet another life. Sorted!
Nevertheless! This time, with absolute awakening of the self.
All set to merge into the cosmic oneness!

11. EARTH

A giant blue ball swirling on and on.
Holding its unique features intact with its spaces.
Gripping all creatures, with her own gravity of lovable nature.
Revolving around the sun being her all time passion.
No shakes and turns, affecting her lovable children in fashion.
The five major elements being the source of existence.
Whereas, land being the source of rigid body.
Water being the source of flow.
Air being the source of action.
Fire being the source of transformation.
Space being the source of mind.
Lies the primordial nature of the creator.
Existing in all the creations with its own everlasting chime!

12. THE SUN

Occupying the center of the vast system.
All the planets revolving around you at a permeable distance.
Nothing can near you, though close you may seem.
You being the enormous source of energy for all beings.
Your marvelous motion, sparkling in the enormous darkness.
Reminds me of my source of real existence.
Penetrating into the duality of action and stillness.
You are absolutely active yet still!
Two extremes merging with absolute will.
A Stunning glowing golden sphere.
Such an enormous view of sight.

13. ILLUSION

Sunrise and sunset, such a delightful sight to admire.

As our eyes witness the rise and fall of the red hued ball.

Yet the fact unfolds, the true static nature of its being.

Only the earth rotating around on a particular axis around.

Creating such a huge difference in vision.

Misleading our own knowledge of existence.

Truth hidden beneath, unmoved and untouched.

Is the world itself functioning on an illusional theme?

Even the shiny silvery moon, falling in the same illusive loop.

Growing and fading at times in a frame.

Yet standing full without any change.

Everything has begun with the law of perception.

From Latitudes and Longitudes, and all directions.

Concepts born out of human excellence.

To enhance human's nature of life on earth.

Giving birth to beliefs and systems full-fledged.

Forgetting the real bond of nature as such.

Getting driven by the traditional customs bound.

And here we are into the illusive world fully drowned!

14. CHAIN OF SPECIES

Knowledge about the world keeps changing now and then.
Change being the only permanent trend.
On the whole, we have lost the universal blend.
Of living a fruitful life and gaining a never ending end.
Though we share our lives with all these existing creatures.
Our difference of opinions and dominance in mind.
Leading to mere abduction and ruining some domain.
Agitating our inner mind, creates violence in the outer world.
One last thing to remember at all times.
We are all just a part of this ever ending chain.
Mutually connected with one and another.
Nothing divides us from the universal main.
Apart from our own defensive and self-destructive brain.
Moving far away from the center, leading us in vain.
Boozing our minds with no finite gain!

15. AWARENESS

Awareness being the ardent nature of the "Self".
Through which one sorts out his inner quest.
Awareness paving the real finite way.
One fetches the way to explore the hidden treasures.
Making our hearts bloom with "Innocence".
Clearing away the clouds of "Ignorance".
Bringing forth the reality of "Existence".
"Acceptance" being a boon to human excellence.
Perseverance being its ultimate essence.
Breaking the rigid inner boundaries.
Like a galloping horse that strides, fast into its path.
Our life blends with the buoyant flow.
Bringing about an exceptional balance.
Unveiling the heart center of life!

16. KNOWLEDGE

Knowledge is all about knowing.
Knowing being a state of action, occurring in the present.
Where knowledge becoming the data of that particular action.
Knowing is tremendous, as it just fills your heart.
While storing up of the knowledge without execution.
Can burden up your mind, pressuring your heart.
"Whatever you know, is not who you are".
Instead, "Whatever you do, marks the real you".
"Emptiness" bringing forth "Acceptance".
Only when you are empty, you can be filled.
Filling and emptying,the ultimate process of mental excavation.
What you fill, has to be emptied, in order to fill anew.
Constant thinking of an action, without execution, is of no use.
Knowledge into action, brings forth the real transformation.
While piling up of knowledge leads to "Arrogance".
Stagnating the flow of life, in the same phase loosing vitality.
And thereby falling into the loop of time ,delaying growth!

17. ACTION AND REACTION

Every action has its own innate reaction.

We react accordingly to our observed and absorbed action.

Absorption of situations, leading to emotional stimulation.

Taking multiple roles in the drama of life.

We react according to the point of our observance.

Observance being the basal matter for absorption.

But awareness standing beyond observance.

Awareness being the state of actual existence.

You will be aware of both your actions and your reactions.

Understanding being the foundation for every reaction.

Emotions are intricate inner wirings.

Through which the output of reaction takes place.

We dwell into plenty of emotions in and out.

As we grow, we learn to deal, with all sorts and stuffs.

18. MATURITY

A toddler is a toddler until he reaches three.
On becoming a preschooler he explores with his new friends, free.
While an adult realizes his phase of growth.
Taking the whole responsibility, as a state of maturity.
No matter whether good or bad.
Either you can handle or not.
Taking responsibility is itself an act of maturity.
Only when you try, you learn new things a while.
Either you flaunt or you fail.
Learning is mere growing, which nurtures your state of being.
Every process of learning accompanying an experience of yourself.
Only when you fall, you start to rise.
Success is not at the end of accomplishment.
The journey preaching the whole essence.
Ultimately your goals extend when the poles are reached.
Only the journey matters on the whole.

19. BALANCE

Life is merely a two sided coin.

With every action, its own reactions on.

As light vanishes the darkness around.

Stillness stimulating the motion surround.

Good and bad equilibrant to each other.

Mind being magnetized and attracted to either.

Like anode and cathode being the dual ends of a battery.

Distinguished by a central neutral line.

Balancing the positive and negative.

Bringing forth the state of neutrality.

Whereas neutrality being equilibrant.

Evolving into the dual branches of positive and negative.

Like the nucleons balancing the state of every atom.

Apart from the protons and electrons.

The state of neutrality being the root existence of every being.

20. NATURE OF THE SELF

"LOVE" being the innate nature of the self.
The purity of which that cannot be altered.
Purely existing with its impartial nature.
Hidden deep, beneath the illusive nature.
Constraining its flow, by the inner built boundaries.
Love is an inner state of transformation.
Flourishing deep inside a being, with respect to "Self".
Beyond the mental agendas established.
As of the pure love between a mother and her baby.
You evolve out of love.
You get a form out of love.
It is the only purest and highest form of human nature.
Uniting human with all form of creatures.
A balanced mind pertains the flow of love.
Only out of love we shall merge into the flow of life.

21. THE POWER OF BELIEF

Belief being the basic survival instinct of human.
Your life starts with belief.
You crawl and step up and run with the belief in you.
Children believe so strongly and pursue their needs effortlessly.
They don't care as they fall.
They rise ahead and play with all.
But as we mature we lose the ability to believe.
Conditioning our mind and losing the ability to expand.
As we keep on, loading our minds.
With all sorts of information and emotions gained.
Gradually moving away from the flow of belief,
Making our inner "Self" too rigid.
Thoughts into belief brings forth action and execution.
Belief being the basic essential to deal any situation.
"Life packed with whole lot of possibilities"
No way is similar to that of the other.
Each one exploring his own way of sorting problems.
Depending on their ability to believe in their own "Self".
Each one acquires his own key from the universe.
To unlock and explore new doors ahead !

22. THE PATH

Each and everyone in this world, explores their own path.
Each one's path is so unique, as that of our faces on earth.
You are the ruler of your life until you realize this verse right.
Ultimately you blend with the flow of life.
When the path reveals itself to you.
You might wonder abound, after its revelation.
As all the twists and turns in life are just the way of your path.
Life like a ride on a rollercoaster.
All the ups and downs heading to the safe point of start.
Life seems complicated when your mind is full of with thoughts.
Once you take over the charge, your mind is in your incharge.
Everything falls into right place, as of never before.
Life being a beautiful journey with escalating opportunities.
To explore, enhance, emphasis and expand one's own self.
To attain the highest form of human excellence.

23. MIND

Mind like a beautiful garden.
With raw soil that can be sowed of any sort.
What you sow, is what you reap.
Awareness being the owner of the garden.
And the five senses being its door into it.
The seeds are sowed through the five senses.
What all you see, hear, feel, sniff and sense.
Getting a default sow in the garden of mind.
Like the seeds of belief, fear, anger, confidence and expectation.
And the list goes. on and on filling all the spaces.
Only through mere awareness you take incharge of your garden.
At first you may tremble upon its maintenance.
Later by practicing you might got to know of its significance.
Transforming it into a beautiful garden.
Nurturing fruits and flowers.
Sharing and caring with the fellow beings.

24. SELF LOVE

The nature of pure love begins from the self.
"Self-love" an eminent key,to unlock the doors of your garden.
Prioritizing yourself, changes the dimensions of your life.
A thin line distinguishing the egoistic self and the real self.
Egoistic self shall ruin the garden with its pride .
The real self nutures, creating a symphony in life.
Self-love reverberates the pattern of nature .
Blending you smoothly,to embrace the unfolding moments of life.
Journey being valued so much than that of your destination.
When you love your self,you care for others too.
You become pliable giving birth to empathy.
Just like a language through which, you commune with someone.
Your inner environment takes control over the outer too.
Self-love being an independent stream.
Does not acquire any external beam.
Being aware of your thoughts now and then.
Shall train your inner glen.
Love that flourish,shall flow through the valleys of life.
Making you dance to the rhythm of life.
Every change starts with you.
Every change is a treasure gained !

25. CHANGE

Change being the ultimate source of your energy center.
A constant movement of push and pull towards the stream of life.
Your inner potential like a ball of energy.
As you adapt change your ball grows abundantly.
While you restrict change, your ball begins to shrink.
A good beginning always possess a good ending.
Good sleep the previous night, begins day bright.
Every change may seem hard at start.
But once you catch the spine, you merge with its flow.
At times you realize, change is not a separate thing.
"You yourself is the change".
Change sculpts the irregularities into an unique masterpiece.
Adapting to change emphasizes your growth.
From a small ball of energy expanding into a huge mass.
As the ball grows bright, it lightens up all sides !

26. HABITS - SMALL STEPS TO CHANGE

Habits being the small little footsteps in your journey of life.
"Who you are is what you practice."
Habits aiding you to redefine yourself.
Leading you into the world full of possibilities.
Leaping you against the hurdles of impossibilites.
Fear being born out of the lack of trust in your own ability.
Constraining yourself within a particular boundary.
Habits move your boundaries beyond the scope of expectations.
Breaking all the inner walls of fear, failure, and immobility.
Revealing your actual ability and transforming your potentiality.
By taking one steady step at a time, change is accomplished.

27. DISCIPLINE

Discipline being the root of a successful habit.
By creating and maintaining a healthy routine.
Our inner and outer environment is sculpted.
Paving the right way for a better future.
Discipline is not about controlling or restraining your own self.
To something that you distaste.
Discipline merely born out of passion and concentration.
The love to embrace the change in you.
Regulating your daily flow of thoughts and actions.
Helping mind to calm down in situations.
Emphasizing and expanding your true potential.
Beyond your known knowledge of your "Self".
What we all know about us or the world is too little,
Delve deep into the ocean of experience without any brittle.
Organizing yourself saves much time.
"A disciplined mind is a powerful tool born out of practice".

28. BE THE RULER OF YOUR "SELF"

Boundaries are formed only out of the known.
If you think "you can", it happens actually as planned!
And if you think "you cannot", it stops at the moment of start.
Consistently conditioning your mind, restrains the flow.
Creating a temporary illusional phase, deserted alone.
Tremendous flow of expansion occurring now and then.
Journey being the actual purpose at the end.
To rule is to live, beyond the mental boundaries, that fetch ill.
To live in the present, being the only profound action.
That one attains through complete awareness.
With which, one entirely takes over his own kingdom of the self.
As your way deepens, the waves gets soften.
Revealing your inner potential in reality.

29. PRESENT

Present, the only existing phase of all times.
Being the birth place of reality and truth.
Where you merge, with the instant flow of life.
Past and future being the dual branches of the present.
Present actions, the root of the past and upcoming future as well.
To be in the present, is to come "out of the judgemental
situation".
Were mind getting attracted to the situations around.
Dwelling into the situation, blinds your inner alarm .
And we feel constrained in the situation, without any clue.
Thoughts flood regretting the past or fearing about the future.
Losing the precious moments of the lively present .
When you think hard, you scatter far.
Creating sequence of thoughts in loop.
Over thinking, never a solution, as it drains your whole energy.
Making you stumble,without any clear decisions.
Thoughts flow according to the nature of observance.
Changing your attitude,shall reveal the hidden truth beneath.
Glancing at situations, as a mere audience.
You gain the power of "witnessing" your own life.
The role aiding you to blend into the present.
Avoiding any emotional unwanted attachments.

Mind unveiling the reasons, behind each and every situation.
You stay astound at the sight of the truth where the present leads.
Entirely calm and composed in the present, without even a
snout.

30. DECLUTTER YOUR MIND

Decluttering your mind saves tremendous energy and time.
By limiting your thoughts abound.
Creating an inner balance over any situation around.
Thoughts stream out in the valley of time.
Continuously expanding in the absence of awareness.
Awareness being the central source of the self.
Segregating the flow of thoughts aside.
Making the space of mind clutter free.
Eliminating all unwanted, things piled up flee.
When mind is free, you become pliable in all fields.
Where things seems to happen without any frustration.
"Breathe" being an invincible key.
To keep your mind clutter free !

31. JUST BREATHE

Concentration of your breath, ends all your stress.
Renouncing all your thoughts, at a stretch.
Concentration is to see as such without any aim.
As you travel with the flow of your piling thoughts,
Your concentration actually becomes scarce.
Thoughts keep filling our mind, unavailable for concentration.
"The golden rule for concentration, free mind without emotion."
You concentrate to comprehend things happening around.
Entering the zone of judgement, puts an end to concentration.
Building inner boundaries, restricts any change to occur.
Making you stagnate in the same situation over and over.
Concentration strengthens, your charging phase of mind.
Enabling your mind to be actively present with pure awareness.
When stream of thoughts floods over, your mind becomes restless.
Concentrating the flow of your breath.
Helps you calm afresh and overcome the stress!

32. THE JUDGEMENT ZONE

We keep on judging our own-self and others.

Judging being either the product of past stored,

Or preconception of the upcoming future.

We judge people, according to their actions in the past.

Change being predominant nature of the universe.

People do change and so as we.

Non-judgmental imparts a nature of "acceptance".

No matter of who and what they were.

We accept and embrace them as such at present.

Were we care and share, the flow of our love.

With all fellow beings, existing at present.

"All change roots from within, as the soil is one's mind."

Like the glow of a candle, illuminating light on all sides.

Our rigid judgemental matter, melting into plasmic feature.

Making life glow effortlessly with flow.

33. DESIRE

A healthy desire, being the need of the hour.
Which will never make, you fall apart.
A desire born out of cunningness and greed.
Shall end up putting you, in the brim of suffering.
Desires being pure wishes, one needs.
Building hopes and motives serving the actual purpose.
While crossing the faint line, shall lead into disaster.
Where hopes and happiness vanishes at flee.
Piling up sufferings for free.
All our needs shall be fulfilled, with utmost care.
As of the mother's loving nature, for child's welfare.
If it hurts, you suffer and then you wake up, into a state.
Were you recognize the step misplaced.
Trespassing the line of greed ahead!
Once you are aware, you are out of the trap.
Back into the enormous flow of life bound with love.

34. RELATIONSHIP

Meaningful is the life, when you create a connection with it.
The quality of life merely depending , upon the relationship.
The relationship with persons, things and all sort of patterns.
Marks the quality of the life lived.
To value things or persons you possess.
By developing a pure quality of selfless thoughts.
Every time when a thought is born prioritizing your view.
You move into the egoistic zone, far away from your real "Self".
Impartial being the true nature of the "Self".
Destroying all the conditions around.
Believing and resting in the Nature's womb.
Valuing every relationship sculpts you into a pliable being.
Deep into the valley where the true "Self" abides.
Taking things granted, shall deplete your inner empire.

35. BONDING

Bonding is bipolar imparting mutual concern.
When you are bonded to an object or a person.
It provokes expectation, interrogation and responsibility.
Bonding makes you constrained, with the person or an object.
While love is beyond bonding.
It flows out abundantly without concern of receiving.
Love is pure and it flows without expectation and interrogation.
Having no root of fear.
But bonding imparts a fear of losing.
And it seems hard to let go of any mishappening.
Love being beyond all these boundaries.
To love is to live, with utmost freedom of the illusive self.

36. EXPLORATION OF THE SELF

Humans follow a set of rituals or systems.

Formulated afore a certain period of time.

Later navigating to another system replacing the former.

This being the nature of human hopping from one to another.

Where you keep on experimenting with the do's and dont's.

Preaching upcoming generations to follow the steps blindly.

Without any introspection of the self.

Blinding their own inner vision over reality.

Dumping their limits behind the bars.

Each and every human being unique in their features.

They have their own way to explore this innate nature.

Huge is the necessity to discover one's own way.

As none can follow and replicate any other.

Everyone is unique with their own inner potentiality.

Discover your own passion and resonate in the rhythm of life.

Getting addicted to customs and belief systems ,roots only fear.

Abducting the real freedom of self-exploration.

37. WHEN THINGS FALL APART

There are times when things fall apart.
Failing to set in places as thought.
Pulling you down so hard.
Vanishing all your hopes, built so far.
But nothing can be ruined all of a sudden.
As there is always a light at the end of the tunnel.
Possibilities are numerous with multiple combinations.
When first doesn't work, just go for the next.
Yet nothing is finished, unless you fix your mind set.
Always better give a try, before you think to quit.
Just feeding the mind with the opposite emotion.
Guides you to come out of any drowning situation.
All things happen in a pattern though,
Unlocking the pattern, sways away the delusive low.

38. RESTLESS MIND

A restless mind the perfect place to experiment your way out.
When none comes for rescue, after a huge fall.
Be your own savior and raise to stars!
All emotions being balanced with its opposite pair.
Though hard to consume, the truth stands still.
The world around and the mind within plays an illusive game.
A mere spark illuminating your inner way.
Situations not only teaches but also prepares for future.
Dealing life independently without any ones norms.
Is itself a powerful arm.
You realize the path,overcoming the drowning situations alive.
You being the victim, actor and creator of the play.
Calming your mind ,shall embark your vision.

39. SUFFERING

Suffering being common for every human.
Situations vary, the emotions blurry.
Suffering and pleasure blended with each other.
"When suffering rings, fortune comes!"
But as humans misconceives, suffering prolongs.
Calmness after every storm, being the pattern of nature.
When you suffer you cry out in pain.
Which releases the unwanted stains.
Cleansing you now and then with turns and bends.
As the flow of river that ever ends.
River meets the sea turning into an estuary.
Everything ends with a great change of transformation.
Every end turning into a new beginning!

40. NO PAIN NO GAIN

Every task seems harder at start.
As you break your boundaries of comfort apart.
Preparing your mind being the primary task.
With which you take hold of the path.
Concentrate more on the journey behalf.
Rather than the place of destiny of thought.
Hard times come and go as such.
Sowing numerous seeds within your self.
Hidden seeds take time to bloom.
Belief and patience needed for growth.
You learn through your process of pain.
As reality blooms, you gain.
Embracing the push and pull.
As a tender breeze, swaying the bud.
You rejoice in the rhythm of life !

41. BELIEVE IN YOURSELF

No similar days, fall in a trail.
Everyday blooming anew and frail.
Teaching you the real hidden ability of yourself.
We judge ourselves so quickly than that of others.
As we were brought up in such a societal structure ahead.
Each and every situation carving new depths.
Sculpting our innerself beyond our own efforts.
Experience preaching the real ethics of life.
Unveiling the real tendencies beneath.
To "believe in yourself" being the constant lesson of life.
At times when human mind fails to execute wise.
Tuning your mind with all the possible sights.
Belief illuminating the way of life.
You travel far with no loss of power.

42. BLANK STATE OF ACCEPTANCE

At times when reality, unveils its true nature.
Quite hard to accept, without any curvature.
Faith being the only key to master.
You start to accept, the situation alter.
As you accept, the way brightens broader.
With a tremendous flow of energy further.
Healing your wounds and scars of hurt,
Paving the right way assert.
Acceptance happens when the mind is blank.
Out of any restrictions or questions in demand.
Time being prolonged with grief afore.
All of a sudden, vanishes into thin air as breeze.
Every problem has its own solution, packed up permeably.
Yet life plays the game of hide and seek.
Training mind to seek the hidden truth !

43. THE TRUTH

Truth is monotonous and eternal.
Though conflicts create blockage of vision.
Truth is beneath each and every situation.
By constant endurance and patience of the self.
Truth unveils itself from the heart of reality.
Nothing is permanent until you think so.
Mind loops over the crisis, trenching on external surface.
Letting go of the situation, tunes your mind.
Penetrating deep into the depths of reality.
Where the lustrous pearl of truth is shining.
Amidst the depths of the ocean.

44. BABY MIND

Calm and peaceful is a mind of a baby.
Rejoicing lively all the tiny moments of life.
With heart filled happiness all over.
Spreading unconditional love to gather.
A tender touch of the little one,
Shall relieve thousand unknown pains.
As their storage of memories in mind are so scant.
They rejoice happily like a fly of bird.
As we grow we learn and store ideas and concepts.
Filling our mind with too much loads.
Burdening our heart with baggage of past.
As we grow, our baggage grow.
Letting go of few things apart.
Shall help us regain the weightless nature of baby's heart.
With a pure gaze of sight at all instants of life.

45. THE ART OF LETTING GO

Letting go merely a therapy to heal.
Where our mind needs some space to heal.
Storing up of certain memories of your past.
Burdens your life straining your heart.
Putting your future in vain.
Practicing the art of letting go.
Shall flourish the inner space of soul.
Paving the way to experience life to its fullest.
At times sharing evokes reliving past again in the present.
Draining your whole energy, rooting the same old memory.
Stop thinking of the past that cannot be changed.
Focusing your mind into the current stream of situation.
Life is simple when approached with a dimple.
Life strains when approached with pain.

46. PRACTICE SCULPTS

Practicing few healthy routines, expands your mind's ability.
You become what you practice.
As cleanliness gives pleasure.
A clear mind is unperturbed, with any sort of displeasure.
Disciplining your mind creates a tidy inner environment.
Putting all things in the right place of order.
Levitating the space of mind, experiencing beyond border.
You practice what you understand.
Never forcing others to follow your stands.
Instead, embracing others to explore their own stands.
Exploration beginning at any mere instant.
Though we all live on the same plane of existence.
Situations and reactions vary afar.
Each ones journey being different, on their own path.

47. IGNITE YOUR INNER SELF

Igniting your inner self, creates an everlasting glow.
Self-ignition being the reward for your utmost concentration.
Gaining the vision of your travel, towards destination.
Every human born on earth has their own mission
To be accomplished before the date of expiration.
At times, when clouds of darkness hide your vision.
Tune your mind, it's just a temporary state of fission.
You will regain your awareness after certain tension.
As universe itself, is in a constant movement.
Wait until the clouds clear and again you bear!

48. SHADOW

Darkness being the pure form of existence.
Dancing beyond the duos of light and shadow.
Only when light falls on an object, shadow forms.
Absence objects, sense no forms.
Shadow being a part of the darkness.
Yet darkness standing out as mere existence,
With constant movement of stillness.
Sun being the closest star and the source of light.
Illuminating its light, all over the planets sight.
Though the glow of moon, stunning at night.
Only reflects, a part of sun's light.
Earth being the middle object upright.
Giving birth to a shadowy night.
Though night is dark, it's just a shadow part.
As the real darkness existing beyond the sun,
the moon, the earth and the stars apart.
Is that the place where creations spark?
From such an infinite vast!
Where the truth of stillness and movement is quenched!

49. STILLNESS IN MOTION

An agitated mind is never still.
Reacting to the chain of thoughts, scattering apart.
A trained mind being calm and composed.
Of all the rushes wobbled over.
A gentle sway, clearing all the troubles away.
When silence fetch still, stillness stretch.
Into the center of creation.
Beyond the loop of time and space.
Where it all began being the end.
Constant movement with magnetizing stillness.
The point of merge of all extremes.
Into the path where path is not apart.
Into the infinite beginning!
Into the formless form!
Into the source of truth.
STILLNESS OF WORDS ABOUND!

50. TIME IS NOW

Time being a man-made theory created to enhance life on earth.
Now, the value of time being lost at fright.
All new inventions around, occupying our lives.
Time being more materialized, than ever alive.
Inventions are to fulfill human's expectations.
All new gadgets now, occupying and ruining the human's life.
Diminishing the inner ability and dominating all tendencies.
Humans run over and over, to lead a peaceful life.
After so long run, yet running out of time.
Pity! All human minds that says "I have no time".
No time! To take care of its own self.
Wait! The moment pause is NOW!
Just see WHO, WHAT and WHERE you are?
Time being a tool to be used.
Now has taken all over and ruling you.
Losing your own inner self, no use navigating outer spheres.
None other than human is pressurized by time.
Nor the sun that rises or the birds that chirps.
All living along with nature, blending its rhythm of life.
Only we humans though we possess all, still run out of time!

51. SIXTH SENSE

Humans are gifted with six senses.
Though five being common, among other beings in nature.
One peculiar sense that stands out, as our signature.
"Is the power of awareness of our self."
None other than humans can be aware of their selves.
Only we humans, roam and name ourselves.
Through awareness we open the doors of the self.
Correlating things and matters as such.
A lion doesn't know that it is a lion.
A life of lion being the same for centuries.
The same applies to all species around.
A fish is a fish, that doesn't even wish to come out of its cliché.
We mighty humans changing now and then since centuries.
Even exploring beyond our living planet to the universe ahead.
Whereas external exploration being infinite.
We thrive so hard to catch it finite.
But our source is inbuilt within our inner self.
And here we are, still unaware of our own true self.

52. THE KNOWN AND THE UNKNOWN

What all we knew is limited.

As we are itself a part, of the boundless unlimited.

We tune with the nature with an inner source astound.

Mind being a space, of an empty ground.

Memories becomes the known around.

Staying away from the unknown that surrounds.

A huge leap into the depth of the unknown.

Is attained only when the garden is well maintained.

Unlocking the doors of the inner world.

Through which we survive and rest ashore.

A deep narrow path expanding simultaneously afar.

Into the rooted path where the source of our creation,

Moving to its own rhythm of existence.

Where all the burdening knowns fly apart.

Here I travel into the unknown as a mere part of it, atlast.

Deepening and expanding the state of consciousness.

Merging with the ultimate source of the unknown reality.

53. CONSCIOUS AND UNCONSCIOUS MIND

As you sleep your still alive.
Though, you are consciously blind a while.
Nevertheless, you live in your dreams so alive.
After awake all the illusions fail.
Leaving a sensible touch on your heart aside.
A hidden mysterious switch separating these two states aside.
Were the two extremes of realities merge.
When your mind shuts, yet still alive.
Like an atom being electrically neutral.
By balancing the number of protons and electrons.
Maintaining stability with the help of neutrons.
When the mind is balanced of the GOOD AND BAD.
Into the phase of NEUTRAL pause.

54. INDEPENDENT SOUL

Born into this earth as an independent soul.
As you grow you become dependent ,abode.
Losing your own ability to rise after a fall.
The fall is not just a fall.
It actually makes you realize your flaws.
Every effort made to change yourself.
Is fueling your mind to be disciplined.
Everyone is unique with their own hidden power.
Mastering your self being the innate purpose of life.
The drama continues until the self is unlocked.
Constant awareness being the key.
Though delusions may hide the truth aside.
We are all a part, travelling the same journey of life.
Until the next call strikes!

55. MEDITATION

Meditation being an act of mediation.
Real meditation occurring in the absence of object.
You meditate to unveil your own innerself.
And not that of any object, person or the concepts known.
As objects create shadows in the path of light.
As you objectify things, ideas or concepts.
You move far apart from the meditative plight.
Losing the stability of your inner self.
Dwelling into a state of illusive self.
Where you start reacting according to the knowns.
Transforming your balanced mind to averse yourself.
The pure rule of meditation, being aware of your breath.
Not to control or restrain its flow.
When you are aware ,you just follow its steps.
Without interfering its rhythmic pattern afresh.
You be guided with your breath ahead.
Here you enter into a meditative state.
Were your tremendously active yet still.

56. SILENCE

Travelling into the phase of silence.

As the mind stops, its mighty chatters after decades of violence.

Silence not being empty and void.

It is a state full of clarity bevoice.

A silent mind is a powerful tool.

To harmonize the inner self with nature's hue.

Letting go of the wanted and unwanted thoughts.

Thriving your mind into the silence path.

The inner beauty revealed, after a magnetizing pass.

Deep into the zone of the magnificent heart.

Silence being the ultimate treasure impart.

Breaking all the dualities, merging with the reality!

Afterword

As we bid farewell to these words our journey does not end here.For life is an ongoing narrative,a story that unfolds each passing day,new experience and fleeting moment.May these verses serve as guideposts illuminating the path ahead,reminding us the beauty and wonder that awaits us!

With gratitude and love,
Vaishnavi Ramesh